A Special
Gift

From

_____

to

_____

Date

_____

ACKNOWLEDGMENT

My peerless wife.

Your contributions to my life and the
ministry has been immeasurable. I'm
forever grateful to God for such a blessing
as you.
For being my best friend, my number one
supporter and life partner.
I love you.

FIFTY
ANCIENT WISDOM
FOR SINGLES

Dr. Daniel Olukoya

50 ANCIENT WISDOM
FOR SINGLES

(c) 2014 DR. D.K. OLUKOYA
ISBN: 978 978 920 0986

A publication of the
Mountain of Fire and Miracles Ministries
International Headquarters, Lagos Nigeria.

All scripture quotations are from the King
James Version of the Bible.
Unless otherwise stated.

INTRODUCTION

Wisdom is the ability to make good and commendable judgement because of one's experience and knowledge. It is the quality of being wise. The Bible speaks a lot about wisdom. Wisdom is very expedient for any child of God who desires to make heaven, to live in this earth, and to fulfill his or her purpose of creation.

There are three types of wisdom present in this world; Godly wisdom, worldly wisdom and satanic wisdom. Godly wisdom from Heaven, are bestowed by God on His children. The wisdom of this world emanates from the natural thinking ability of man while the satanic wisdom emanates from the kingdom of darkness, and it's motivated by satan. The wisdom of this world tells you that as an individual, you can become whatever you want to become and achieve whatever you want to achieve but the satanic wisdom will go some extra miles by saying you can do all things without the knowledge and supervision of God.

The wisdom of man has led many people to hell-fire and unredeemable errors. Although about 90percent of the world population live according to the wisdom of this world, yet the role divine wisdom plays can never be ignored. Unfortunately, even the so-called Christians in the world today operate their lives according to the dictates of worldly wisdom. There is a big need for Christians to buckle up and brace themselves for the ever-unfolding surprises this world has to offer. Anyone who refuses to move along will certainly be left behind. Moreover, if anyone desires to live as a Christian in this world, which is fraught with so much deception, torment, trouble, he or she can only operate by the wisdom of God.

50

Ancient Wisdom

1

INAPPROPRIATE DRESSING WILL ATTRACT WORTHLESS PARTNERS.

Pleasing the Lord with your attires simply means you need to consider the purpose for which God created you, and then dress accordingly whenever you are dressing yourself up. This is very important.

INAPPROPRIATE DRESSING WILL ATTRACT WORTHLESS PARTNERS.

If you are the type of single individual who dresses without giving thought to moral and biblical standards, then you have inadvertently concluded to attract members of the opposite sex that are likewise undesirable and worthless. As a matter of fact, your dressing says a lot about you and your personality.

There is so much confusion and perversion all over the world and in the society today due to what can be termed 'presentation' or what is now jokingly referred to as 'packaging'. That is, how individuals perceive and present themselves, especially in the area of clothing. A particular designer, at a time, openly said on air that 'every dressing and design has a voice and language that speaks'. So anyone that wears any attire is giving a specific and direct message of the design to the people looking at him or her. I therefore encourage you to clothe yourself to please the Lord and not just anybody.

Pleasing the Lord with your attires simply means you need to consider the purpose for which God created you, and then dress accordingly whenever you are dressing yourself up. This is very important.

By God's standards, there are recommendations for your dressing.

As ladies, you should dress with the intent to cover your nakedness. Women that dress skimpily and go on the street will definitely attract the kind of men that go after such mode of dressing: lustful and wanton men. They will only get attracted to the carnal thing they want from such misguided women.

To avoid being confused, there are some biblical recommendations about how we, as believers, should dress. These are found in the following Bible passages.

1 Timothy 2:9-10: Likewise also that women should adorn themselves in respectable apparel, with modesty and self-control, not with braided hair and gold or pearls or costly attire, but with what is proper for women who profess godliness—with good works.

1 Corinthians 6:19-20: Or do you not know that your body is a temple of the Holy Spirit within you, whom you have from God? You are not your own, for you were bought with a price. So glorify God in your body.

Deuteronomy 22:5: A woman shall not wear a man's garment, nor shall a man put on a woman's cloak, for whoever does these things is an abomination to the Lord your God.

1 Peter 3:3: Do not let your adorning be external—the braiding of hair and the putting on of gold jewelry, or the clothing you wear.

2

YOU ENTER INTO A COVENANT WITH WHOSOEVER DEFLOWERS YOU.

In most cases; the marital delays we often talk about and witness today came about as a result of the blood covenants that were formed with first sexual partners that were not broken.

YOU ENTER INTO A COVENANT WITH WHOSOEVER DEFLOWERS YOU.

When a man deflowers a woman, a blood covenant is formed. This is because the blood from the broken maidenhead or hymen of the woman wets the male copulatory organ of the man, and by this act, a blood covenant is activated. I want to let you know that this transcends the physical; it is purely a spiritual matter. That is why it is good for singles to keep their virginity until they are married because the first man that had sex with them has a big role to play in their life. If the man or woman you are about to marry now is not the man who deflowers you, then you have a blood covenant to break before you can peacefully go on with your marital life.

In most cases, the marital delays we often talk about and witness today came about as a result of the blood covenants that were formed with first sexual partners that were not broken. Also the spiritual content of the first partner is very important. If the man involved in the covenant is sexually loose, the lady too will be sexually loose. If the man is an evil person as a first sexual partner, he will definitely deposit evil seed in the lady which will make her evil too.

If you are a man and you are among those that believe it is a macho thing to be sleeping around like a dog and you have deflowered a lot of ladies, you are in real trouble because the blood covenants you formed with each of these ladies will trouble you. This is a serious spiritual matter. If you don't deal with it in your own life, it will extend to your children and an evil cyclical pattern will be formed. This is why deliverance is most necessary for such persons to break the yoke involved in this bondage.

3

A REAL MAN WILL NEVER ASK FOR SEX BEFORE, OR OUTSIDE MARRIAGE.

The ripe time for any sexual intercourse, or any sexual contact for that matter, is after he has lawfully taken his wife to the altar and they are properly wedded in the presence of God's people.

A REAL MAN WILL NEVER ASK FOR SEX BEFORE, OR OUTSIDE MARRIAGE.

If you are engaged, or you are in courtship with someone who demands for sex, you have not found a future spouse yet but a playboy or a Casanova. A real man and a true believer will not be angling for sex before or outside marriage knowing that it is against the commandment and instruction of God. Rather, he will be patient until the time is ripe for it. The ripe time for any sexual intercourse, or any sexual contact for that matter, is after he has lawfully taken his wife to the altar and they are properly wedded in the presence of God's people.

This means as a believer, premarital and extra marital affairs (when married) are a no-no area for you.

4

THE TIME YOU SPENT WITH THE WRONG SET OF PEOPLE IS DESTINY-WASTED.

If you do not have good friends, invest your time in reading good books that are written by great authors.

THE TIME YOU SPENT WITH THE WRONG SET OF PEOPLE IS DESTINY-WASTED.

It is a well-known fact that life is a function of time, and fulfilling your earthly destiny depends on how, and with whom, you spend that valuable time. Time is the only resource in life that can never be regained if lost or frittered away. So you must learn how to invest time with good people in meaningful and healthy relationships. As a single intending to enter into marriage, if your major friends are unbelievers, drunkards, club-goers, laggards, ne'er-do-wells, prostitutes, liars, gamblers, et cetera, then you are gradually but surely sabotaging your own marital destiny.

If you do not have good friends, invest your time in reading good books that are written by great authors. By so doing, you enrich your mind and your thinking faculty is vastly improved. When the time comes to make good decisions, you will be ready to make good and binding decisions that will impact your destiny.

5

DO NOT MARRY FROM WHERE YOU ARE COMING FROM; RATHER, MARRY FROM WHERE YOU ARE GOING TO.

Marry a man whose prayer life will challenge and uplift you and never otherwise.

DO NOT MARRY FROM WHERE YOU ARE COMING FROM; RATHER, MARRY FROM WHERE YOU ARE GOING TO.

You must endeavor to marry someone who will take or lead you to your destined end. You must not be ignorantly yoked in marital relationship with someone just because he or she has the fortuitous 'blessing' of coming from your village, former university, tribe, ethnic group or church. No.

The reason for this is because these are places where you are coming from. Your determination should be to marry someone who will take you from where you are now to where God wants you to be. Do not make the mistake of marrying a man you are begging to pray. Rather, marry a man whose prayer life will challenge and uplift you. If you are in courtship with somebody who is allergic or pervious to prayers, no matter how caring he is, you had better run. This is because the real nature of a man or a woman is seen in the spiritual, and actions and reactions to sincere spiritual activities reflect who a person truly is.

In summary, you must have a purpose before a partner. This means that when you discover and know your divine purpose in life, the journey to getting the partner who will play a major role in fulfilling this purpose becomes easy.

6

PRESSURES AND ANXIETIES ARE
INTELLIGENT ROBBERS THAT
MAKE PEOPLE TO EMBRACE
COUNTERFEITS AND SUBSTITUTES.

Decisions taken under pressure
always backfire in the end.

PRESSURES AND ANXIETIES ARE INTELLIGENT ROBBERS THAT MAKE PEOPLE TO EMBRACE COUNTERFEITS AND SUBSTITUTES.

If everyone around you is putting pressure on you to marry because, according to them, you are due, or overdue, and you allow that pressure to enter into your head and compel you to make bad decisions, you will surely miss your road and you alone are culpable. Decisions taken under pressure always backfire in the end. It always results in the person marrying a wrong partner, and this factor alone accounts for many marriage failures and divorce rates. The best thing to do under this condition is to prayerfully wait on God and disregard all ungodly sympathizers who can lead one astray.

The case of Abraham in the Bible is a good example of waiting on God for a desired thing. His passive acceptance of his wife's choice of Hagar as a surrogate or substitute wife led to the birth of a child who was not the fulfillment of God's promise. Our present world is still reeling under the effect of this unwise and pressured choice.

7

WHEN A COURTSHIP HAS AN
EVIDENCE OF VIOLENCE OR A BAD
HABIT WHICH IS NOT WORKED
UPON, IT IS A POINTER THAT THE
MARRIAGE IS HEADING FOR THE ROCKS.

Your experiences during courtship
will give you the signals on how
things will be in the marriage.

7

WHEN A COURTSHIP HAS AN EVIDENCE
OF VIOLENCE OR A BAD HABIT WHICH IS
NOT WORKED UPON, IT IS A POINTER
THAT THE MARRIAGE IS HEADING
FOR THE ROCKS.

If, during the courting period, the man is already dishing out slaps and pummeling the lady, or the lady is already exposing the young man to open disgrace, then the two are gradually walking into a hell while still on earth. If the man smokes and during the courtship, the lady discovers, and he tells her that it is an accident and begs with an innocent face, and the lady gets carried away with his sweet talks, and easily pushes the issue under the carpets, the lady should not be surprised if, after the marriage proper, the man graduates to sniffing cocaine and marijuana.

8

IT IS THE DUTY OF THE MAN TO FIND AND TO PROPOSE, NOT THE LADY.

Conversely, when you, as a lady, go to propose to a man yourself, you cheapen yourself before him and there might be unsavoury consequences.

IT IS THE DUTY OF THE MAN TO FIND AND TO PROPOSE, NOT THE LADY.

As a lady, you cannot go to a man and tell him you dreamt about him a lot and you think he should be your husband. This is not a wise move at all. Any man who cannot come to you to propose that he wants to marry you is not a real man, and cannot be a good husband that is worthy of your hand in marriage.

Conversely, when you, as a lady, go to propose to a man yourself, you cheapen yourself before him and there might be unsavoury consequences. As a matter of fact, the lady might be snubbed, shunned, scorned or face outright disgrace from the man who might misjudge or misinterpret her intentions.

The Bible has already given the standard to be followed: the man is the one that does the finding. You should also take note of something very instructive here. The Bible emphasizes 'finding' and not 'seeing'. This suggests that some proactive moves are involved.

9

PAY GOOD ATTENTION TO
YOUR APPEARANCE.

If you are the type that dresses
care-free, people will wonder whether
you are okay, and you will repel,
rather than attract, members of the
opposite sex.

PAY GOOD ATTENTION TO YOUR APPEARANCE.

As a young and intending bride or bridegroom, you cannot afford to appear anyhow. As a young lady, do not dress like a grandmother or a hag. The fact that you attend a holiness-preaching church, praying church, or a Pentecostal church does not mean you should dress haggardly or tattered. At the Mountain of Fire and Miracles Ministries, we do not encourage haggard dressing, or the wearing of threadbare clothes, especially for intending couples. You cannot wear a jacket and slippers; these do not match. If you are the type that dresses care-free, people will wonder whether you are okay, and you will repel, rather than attract, members of the opposite sex. If you are going for a native wear, avoid oversized ones that will swallow your slender and beautiful frame.

Your entire clothing accessory must be balanced and well-coordinated. For instance, as a lady, the hat that you wear to church should be stylish, to make you look great. Though worldliness is not encouraged, yet we must be neatly and elegantly dressed.

And if you are the type that sweats a lot, get a deodorant to eliminate intolerable odours from your body, especially areas like the armpit region that are not well-exposed to much sunlight or air. Also, if you are the type that has mouth odour, you might need a good mouthwash, or better still, use minty gums to keep your breath fresh.

These are simple nuggets of hygienic wisdom, but they go a long way in defining your personality, and ensuring that a good and lasting impression is made. You should be aware of the popular saying that: 'The first impression lasts longer, and is difficult to change.' In other words, you do not have a second chance to make an impression. It has been found out through research that an impression is made in the first four seconds of meeting a person. People see you before they hear you, and the way you dress determines the way you will be addressed. It doesn't have to be expensive, so pay good attention to your appearance.

10

YOU CANNOT CONVERT SOMEONE TO YOUR FAITH OR BELIEF-SYSTEM IN ORDER TO MARRY HIM OR HER.

The reason this is madness is simply because no human on the surface of the earth has the power to convert another. Conversion, by conviction, is the work of the Holy Spirit.

YOU CANNOT CONVERT SOMEONE TO YOUR FAITH OR BELIEF-SYSTEM IN ORDER TO MARRY HIM OR HER.

This is not only preposterous, but it is also a stupid thing to do. The reason this is madness is simply because no human on the surface of the earth has the power to convert another. Conversion, by conviction, is the work of the Holy Spirit.

A lot of ladies, and men too, fancying themselves in love and desperate to get into marital relationships; have fallen into conjugal errors by entertaining the naïve belief that a spouse can be converted into their own faith after marriage. Many of them have been shocked by the dire consequences that this action resulted into: confused children and broken homes.

11

KEEP YOURSELF PURE AND YOUR BED UNDEFILED.

Before marriage, abstain from sexual sins such as fornication and other promiscuous behaviour at all cost.

KEEP YOURSELF PURE AND YOUR BED UNDEFILED.

Before marriage, abstain from sexual sins such as fornication and other promiscuous behaviour at all cost.

There are some current worldly teachings which are totally strange and are deviations from these laid-down standards of the Bible. They call it 'great grace'. They teach, under this false belief, that once you have already surrendered your life to Jesus, you don't need to care about the sins you commit again, that you are already saved and 'the grace' covers you. These apostates do not take into reckoning the golden words of the scripture that says: 'Shall we continue in sin and say grace should abound?'

A lot of these teachings are erroneous and misleading. They are words of human wisdom and reasoning, and they propagate wrong and false gospels that are leading people to hell fire. You will be most unwise if you follow such apostacy.

12

WEDDING IS A DAY AFFAIR BUT MARRIAGE IS A LIFETIME.

As a single, you need to realize that a wedding is a day affair, but a marriage is for a lifetime. Therefore put your heart and mind on values that endure and not on ephemeral things of the world

WEDDING IS A DAY AFFAIR BUT MARRIAGE IS A LIFETIME.

A lot of money is spent nowadays on doing society weddings but a lot of these weddings are really based on worldly and superficial things, such as family connections, the social status of the parents, the good looks of the couple, and so on, and not on the established Word of God. This often makes the marriage, which is the aftermath of the wedding, to be built on shallow foundations which often crumble like a pack of cards after just few weeks or months.

As a single, you need to realize that a wedding is a day affair, but a marriage is for a lifetime. Therefore put your heart and mind on values that endure and not on ephemeral things of the world, while waiting on God to find a life partner.

13

REMEMBER TO WAGE WAR AGAINST THE DEVIL THAT FOUGHT YOUR PARENTS' MARRIAGE.

This is extremely important as any ancestral or generational curse or covenant that is not broken gives the devil a foothold and a leeway into such marriage.

REMEMBER TO WAGE WAR AGAINST THE DEVIL THAT FOUGHT YOUR PARENTS' MARRIAGE.

Many devils which assailed our parents' marriages, in their own generation, in the form of satanic covenants and curses have to be identified and broken by the intending couple before they can move into their marital destiny. This is extremely important as any ancestral or generational curse or covenant that is not broken gives the devil a foothold and a leeway into such marriage. This will manifest in the form of spirit-wife/spirit-husband issues; barrenness; financial difficulties and chains of poverty; terminal diseases like fibroids; cycle of ill-luck; failure-at-the-edge-of-breakthrough syndrome, et cetera.

14

MARRIAGE IS A COVENANT, SO ALWAYS LOOK BEFORE YOU LEAP.

Once you enter into it, breaking it is a serious problem.

MARRIAGE IS A COVENANT, SO ALWAYS LOOK BEFORE YOU LEAP. .

The marriage institution is a covenanted one, recognized by divine and secular order. It is instituted by God and recognized as a covenant relationship by all the host of heaven. Once you enter into it, breaking it is a serious problem. No matter how you try to break it, the marriage covenant cannot be broken except, when death is adduced as the reason.

15

IT IS BETTER TO WAIT FOR GOD'S TIME
IN MARRIAGE THAN JUMPING INTO
MARRIAGE AT THE DEVIL'S TIME.

During this waiting period, the Lord
works on us - moulds and shapes
us to be more like His son Jesus -
and chisels us to fit into His will.

IT IS BETTER TO WAIT FOR GOD'S TIME IN MARRIAGE THAN JUMPING INTO MARRIAGE AT THE DEVIL'S TIME.

As children of the God, the Most High has a divine agenda and a divine timetable for all His children. The time lapse between the spiritual conceptualization of this agenda, and the physical manifestation, requires from us human beings a waiting period. During this waiting period, the Lord works on us - moulds and shapes us to be more like His son Jesus - and chisels us to fit into His will.

Unfortunately, a lot of God's children, are like Saul at the battle with the Amalekites.

They fail to wait for the full expiration of this term but rather jump into the marriage circuit without adequate or proper consultation with the Owner of the blueprint. The devil, who is the brain behind this premature and unholy union uses the error created to afflict and torment his ignorant victims. You as a single should imbibe the virtue of patience, and hear clearly from God, before you enter into a relationship that will lead into a marital union.

16

IT IS BETTER TO BE SINGLE, BELIEVING
GOD TO BE MARRIED THAN TO BE
MARRIED AND PRAYING TO BE SINGLE.

This untoward situation can be
avoided if singles pray very well
and seek the face of God,
rather than enter into a
matrimonial ceremony they know
little or nothing about.

IT IS BETTER TO BE SINGLE, BELIEVING GOD TO BE MARRIED THAN TO BE MARRIED AND PRAYING TO BE SINGLE.

There is an old saying that: 'marriage is like a place besieged; those without want to get in, while those within wish to get out'. For your information, while thousands of singles like you are looking forward to the day when he or she will be joined in holy matrimony to his or her God-ordained spouse, there are lots of people that are married, but are hoping to become single again. In fact, some of them even pray that their spouses would die so that they could start their lives afresh. The reason for this is because many of them discovered too late that they have a wrong partner, or married into a wrong family. This untoward situation can be avoided if singles pray very well and seek the face of God, rather than enter into a matrimonial ceremony they know little or nothing about.

17

CHILDREN BORN THROUGH FORNICATION OR IMMORAL ACTS WILL NEED DELIVERANCE FROM THE COVENANT OF FORNICATION SO AS NOT TO FOLLOW IN THE STEPS OF THEIR PARENTS.

The case of Jephtah in the Bible is a reminder of the danger inherent in the life of a person who is not fully delivered under the familiar covenant of fornication.

CHILDREN BORN THROUGH FORNICATION OR IMMORAL ACTS WILL NEED DELIVERANCE FROM THE COVENANT OF FORNICATION SO AS NOT TO FOLLOW IN THE STEPS OF THEIR PARENTS.

If your parents never married properly before they gave birth to you, you need to pray hard now so that the same cycle does not repeat for you. The case of Jephtah in the Bible is a reminder of the danger inherent in the life of a person who is not fully delivered under the familiar covenant of fornication. The spirits of error, rejection, unreasonable anger, immorality and bad judgement will continually dog the step of such an individual.

18

GETTING MARRIED IN DARKNESS IS A TRAGEDY.

The fact that you did a church wedding does not mean God is fully 'carried along'. God should be involved and consulted, for His divine

GETTING MARRIED IN DARKNESS IS A TRAGEDY.

This means getting married without divine direction. This is a marriage in which there is no information from heaven; the couple just 'found' each other and carry out a wedding ceremony at which they invite all family members to come and 'chop rice and meat'. This is tragic because the Originator of marriage has been exempted from what He must, of necessity, be involved in. The fact that you did a church wedding does not mean God is fully 'carried along'. God should be involved and consulted, for His divine guidance and approval right from the inception, the point of finding, of making the final decision of who to marry.

19

A BROKEN COURTSHIP IS BETTER THAN A FAILED MARRIAGE.

It's a huge risk to bullishly going ahead into a Godless relationship and risking a failed marriage and a broken home in the future.

A BROKEN COURTSHIP IS BETTER THAN A FAILED MARRIAGE.

This may sound like a trite or common statement but it carries a lot of weight and should not be ignored. Even if the wedding is scheduled for the next day and you receive a divine instruction to back out, it may be difficult, but it is best to obey the divine instruction, rather than bullishly going ahead into a Godless relationship and risking a failed marriage and a broken home in the future.

20

BE A GOOD FRIEND AND YOU WILL ATTRACT TRUE FRIENDS.

If you are a good friend, and people know that you are trustworthy and reliable, word will go round about these desirable traits that you possess.

BE A GOOD FRIEND AND YOU WILL ATTRACT TRUE FRIENDS.

If you are the type that practices 'made-up' or fake Christianity, you will attract people of the same category. You have heard the ancient wisecrack which states that: 'Birds of a feather flock together'. However, if you are a good friend, and people know that you are trustworthy and reliable, word will go round about these desirable traits that you possess and you will attract a commensurate type of friends into your life. As a single, avoid living a lie; do not live a cosmetic life.

21

CARING HEARTS NEVER LACK CARING HANDS.

Among the set of wonderful people that will come your way will be your God-ordained life partner. The example of Ruth suffices.

CARING HEARTS NEVER LACK CARING HANDS.

Once you are a caring person, God will always bring wonderful people along your way that will fill your heart with joy. Among the set of wonderful people that will come your way will be your God-ordained life partner. The example of Ruth suffices. She determined in her heart to follow her mother-in-law to the very end; to care for her, and to fend for her. It was while she was on this heartful work that her marital heavens open and the Lord blessed her with a wonderful husband.

22

FRUSTRATION OFTEN LEADS TO DESPERATION.

Frustration will often lead to desperate acts and desperate actions will lead to catastrophic results.

FRUSTRATION OFTEN LEADS TO DESPERATION.

Never get to a level where you become so desperate, and you don't mind marrying the next person that comes along, or even sleeping with someone simply because you think time is against you. Frustration will often lead to desperate acts and desperate actions will lead to catastrophic results. I pray for you this hour that any power that wants you to be frustrated shall be frustrated by heavens, in the name of Jesus.

23

BAD MARRIAGES CAN BE AVOIDED BEFORE THEY BEGIN.

With the leading of the Holy Spirit and prophetic direction, a bad marriage can be avoided by avoiding a bad courtship.

BAD MARRIAGES CAN BE AVOIDED BEFORE THEY BEGIN.

Avoid bad marriages before they begin. Don't let them start before you start running from pillar to post. You can avoid it! Fortunately for us in this dispensation, the Holy Spirit is available for us. If only we could attune ourselves to His still, small, discernible and audible voice. With the leading of the Holy Spirit and prophetic direction, a bad marriage can be avoided by avoiding a bad courtship. A bad courtship can be avoided by shunning bad habits. Bad habits can be unlearned, and new ones developed.

24

THE BEST WAY TO ENSLAVE A WOMAN IS TO LOVE HER EXCESSIVELY.

Marriage between friends, where love is abundantly showered and laughter flows, often lasts longer.

THE BEST WAY TO ENSLAVE A WOMAN IS TO LOVE HER EXCESSIVELY.

As a rule, women do not run away from where they are appreciated, cherished, loved and pampered. As a single preparing for marriage, pray to God to give you your friend and lover as a spouse in marriage. Marriage between friends, where love is abundantly showered and laughter flows, often lasts longer than one between cohabiting strangers.

25

LOVE IS NOT BLIND BUT INFATUATION AND LUST ARE

As a believing single, avoid emotional or carnal attachment to things of the heart which can lead to spurious and irrational actions.

LOVE IS NOT BLIND BUT INFATUATION AND LUST ARE

Infatuation is a fleeting or a temporary love attraction of one person for another, which is often unrealistic and unreasonable, for instance the emotional rush of a star-struck teenager for her Physics teacher. This is a baseless love which is not enduring at all. It is dangerous to pursue this kind of 'love' because it is blind and not based on reality. As a believing single, avoid emotional or carnal attachment to things of the heart which can lead to spurious and irrational actions. The case to buttress this fact is that of Ahinoam,

David's son; and his half-sister, who he got infatuated with and ended up raping her. He paid for it with his life and caused his father a lot of pain.

26

LOVE PUTS GOD FIRST, LUST PUTS SEX FIRST.

No one that truly loves you wouldn't want to keep you or wait for the right time before asking for sex.

LOVE PUTS GOD FIRST, LUST PUTS SEX FIRST.

Godly love always put Jesus and others first, and itself last. You can easily assess your ongoing relationship with this parameter. If your partner runs after you for sex, lust might be his or her driving wheel and not love. No one that truly loves you wouldn't want to keep you or wait for the right time before asking for sex. If you make love the foundation of your marriage you have just simply signed a contract for a model marriage, a heaven-on-earth experiences.

27

TEST EVERY LOVE WITH YOUR PEACE OF
MIND; IF PEACE OF MIND IS ABSENT,
THERE IS A VERY HIGH PERCENTAGE
THAT GOD IS NOT IN IT.

Put all your relationships to the Power,
Love and Sound Mind test.

TEST EVERY LOVE WITH YOUR PEACE OF MIND; IF PEACE OF MIND IS ABSENT, THERE IS A VERY HIGH PERCENTAGE THAT GOD IS NOT IN IT.

If you are in a relationship and inside of you, there is a sneaking fear which you cannot really explain, wisdom demands that you either wait to clear the cloudiness or you break it up immediately because God is not an author of confusion. Put all your relationships to the Power, Love and Sound Mind test. If they fall short of God's standards, cast them overboard, and trust God for new ones.

28

**MARRIAGE WITHOUT FRIENDSHIP IS
LIKE A SKY WITHOUT SUN.**

Make up your mind to marry your
friend and nothing less.

MARRIAGE WITHOUT FRIENDSHIP IS LIKE A SKY WITHOUT SUN.

In other words, I encourage you to make up your mind to marry your friend and no one else. Most of our parents in the previous generations married their enemies. This resulted in a serious mess that is affecting their children today.

29

IF YOU HURRY INTO MARRIAGE YOU
MAY END UP WITH A PERSON WHO
WILL BURY YOUR DESTINY.

Do not jump into the matrimonial
bandwagon, consider your decision
wisely.

IF YOU HURRY INTO MARRIAGE YOU MAY END UP WITH A PERSON WHO WILL BURY YOUR DESTINY.

As stated somewhere else, pray for, and marry someone who is going in the same direction with you, or better still, someone whose journey in life will help in the fulfillment of your own destiny. Do not jump into the matrimonial bandwagon with someone who will clobber and bury your destiny.

30

A SUCCESSFUL MARRIAGE IS ALWAYS A TRIANGLE.

A thriving marriage is a triumvirate of a man, a woman and God.

A SUCCESSFUL MARRIAGE IS ALWAYS A TRIANGLE.

A thriving marriage is a triumvirate of a man, a woman and God. The center of this relationship is God, who leads, guides and directs through the promptings of the Holy Spirit; followed by the man who receives and executes the Will of God in the marriage, and finally, the woman who encourages, assists and supports the man. As a single who wants marital bliss, this is the model to pray and look forward to.

31

WHY YOU GET MARRIED IS AS IMPORTANT AS WHO YOU MARRY.

It is an aberration for a man to get married and still be dependent on the parents for financial support.

WHY YOU GET MARRIED IS AS IMPORTANT AS WHO YOU MARRY.

Marriage is meant for matured and capable people, and not for boys and girls; those who are matured spiritually, physically, and who are financially and economically empowered and capable of making good decisions. It is an aberration for a man to get married and still be dependent on the parents for financial support. This subjects the man to the whims and caprices of the parents, and if these are unbelieving parents, the man will put his fledging family to unnecessary jeopardy.

It is also unwise to get married just for sexual intercourse. Though this is important as a physical means of expressing love, it is not the ultimate experience in the marital union. Moreover, it has been documented that sexual intercourse gradually diminishes in frequency and potency as the couple gets to know each other over time. This means there is more to entering into the marital relationship than sex. The intending couple has to discover and know which aspect of God's Purpose and Plan they are to fulfill on earth before taking the marital vow.

32

GETTING MARRIED COULD BE EASY BUT STAYING MARRIED IS ANOTHER MATTER ENTIRELY.

You as a single should focus more on those time-tested values that will make you stay married.

32

GETTING MARRIED COULD BE EASY BUT STAYING MARRIED IS ANOTHER MATTER ENTIRELY.

Recent statistics revealed that about fifty to sixty per cent of marriages ended up in divorce during the first five years of consummation. This goes to show that most of the plastic things like wedding cakes, bridal train, 'aso ebi' and other exorbitant displays of wealth during weddings are more often than not, a charade. All these trappings could get them married, quite right, but staying married is another ball game. Unfortunately, a lot of singles nowadays, believers inclusive, have also caught this bug.

On my own wedding day, I got married with just eight people present. We were able, to the glory of God, to overlook much of the frivolous and unnecessary things that people of the world focus their attention on nowadays. Our marriage, which is in its third decade now, was founded on good and cherished Christian principles. You as a single should focus more on those time-tested values that will make you stay married, rather than be mooning for a wedding-day carnival which is built on quicksand.

33

MUCH HAPPINESS IN LIFE DEPENDS
UPON YOUR MARITAL CHOICE.

This is just the simple truth;
try and absorb it for your good.

33

MUCH HAPPINESS IN LIFE DEPENDS UPON YOUR MARITAL CHOICE.

A good choice, a godly match in marriage, will enhance your life, but a bad one will turn your life upside down. That shall never be your portion, in the mighty name of Jesus.

34

A MAN NEEDS DIVINE WISDOM FROM GOD IN CHOOSING WHOM TO MARRY.

God never ignores the sincere cry of His children.

34

A MAN NEEDS DIVINE WISDOM FROM GOD IN CHOOSING WHOM TO MARRY.

Just as God brought Adam's helpmate unto him in the form of Eve, He has predestined a desirable helpmate for all His children. All that we as the apple of His eyes need do, is the wisdom to ask, in the name of His Son Jesus (John 10:10). In due time, He will reveal the right person through any of the diverse means through which He speaks to His children, like dreams, visions, trances, words of knowledge, words of wisdom, prophetic guidance, and so on. He never ignores the sincere cry of His children.

35

DO NOT PLACE YOUR PRIORITIES ON GOOD LOOKS IN YOUR CHOICE OF WHO TO MARRY.

Beauty is subject to individual perspectives. There should be no assertion that anyone is ugly.

DO NOT PLACE YOUR PRIORITIES ON GOOD LOOKS IN YOUR CHOICE OF WHO TO MARRY.

As a matter of fact, no one on this earth is created ugly, by biblical standard. A person may not be up to your taste as an individual. To another fellow, he or she may be the most attractive person. Hence, beauty is subject to individual perspectives. There should be no assertion that anyone is ugly. Beauty is only an ideal in the eye of the beholder. As a single, do not place your major priority on looks when making the choice of who to marry, rather, pray and look for a potential spouse who has the fear of God, which the Bible equates to wisdom. Remember, God does not look at the calf of man, but He is highly interested in the heart of man, where true beauty lies.

36

THE MAJOR CHARACTERISTICS TO LOOK FOR IN A FUTURE PARTNER.

The three most important things to look for in a partner before marriage are the fear of God; discretion, that is, ability to do the right thing at the right time; and godly wisdom.

36

THE MAJOR CHARACTERISTICS TO LOOK FOR IN A FUTURE PARTNER

The three most important things to look for in a partner before marriage are the fear of God; discretion, that is, ability to do the right thing at the right time; and Wisdom. If you are a man, these features should be your ultimate expectations in your spouse and not beauty. The same thing applies to a lady. Beauty and handsome features are good but they will fade away. Good looks and comeliness should be discounted at the expense of godly wisdom. Jesus likened these external traits to a white-painted sepulcher which is attractive on the outside, but internally filled with filthy

and repulsive things. The three traits stated
above are those that will last. They are the
characteristics a wise single must hold tightly
unto.

37

IT IS BETTER TO BE SINGLE AND ALONE
THAN TO BE MARRIED TO THE
WRONG PERSON.

A wrong marriage will cause the regret
that you will give the option to remain
unmarried for life.

IT IS BETTER TO BE SINGLE AND ALONE THAN TO BE MARRIED TO THE WRONG PERSON.

You may be very familiar with this statement but it makes no difference if you have not understood it well. Getting married is not compulsory; just make sure you do not end up in the wrong marriage. This is because a wrong marriage will cause the regret that you will give the option to remain unmarried for life. This shall not be your lot; but it all depends on your decision today.

38

AVOID A WOMAN WHO IS CONTENTIOUS AND ARGUMENTATIVE.

In marital relationships, you fall in love with a person but you have to live with his or her character.

AVOID A WOMAN WHO IS CONTENTIOUS AND ARGUMENTATIVE.

Character is a major factor that determines the future of a marital relationship for good or otherwise. There's even no spiritual counsel that ignores the necessity of a good character person. It is a character disorder when a lady always fights to make her point the topmost in a relationship.

39

THREE MAJOR KINDS OF MEN
TO AVOID ARE

Marriage is beyond the coming
together of two people, it's has to
be properly planned for.

39

THREE MAJOR KINDS OF MEN TO AVOID ARE;

I. Womanizers
ii. Hot-tempered
iii. Drunkard.
If the man is characterized by any of these features, you will never enjoy the marriage.

40

MARRYING A COMEDIAN DOES NOT GUARANTEE A HAPPY MARRIAGE.

There are biblical principles you must follow if your marriage must work.

MARRYING A COMEDIAN DOES NOT GUARANTEE A HAPPY MARRIAGE.

Marriage to an outgoing or a sanguine personality is not a sure-proof bet that the marriage will be successful. You must learn about the biblical principles on how to build a godly home.

41

NEVER BE YOKED WITH ANYONE WHO REFUSES TO BE YOKED TO CHRIST.

he major reason for God's institution of marriage on earth is for His purpose to be fulfilled, and not that of any man's.

41

NEVER BE YOKED WITH ANYONE WHO REFUSES TO BE YOKED TO CHRIST.

A marriage relation between a Christian and an unbeliever is the most disastrous relationship on earth. Although many will argue and claim that they know one or two of such union that are still existing and even successful, these are the exception rather than the norm. The major reason for God's institution of marriage on earth is for His purpose to be fulfilled, and not that of any man's. This Purpose may be defeated when believers are ignominiously yoked with unbelievers in marriage.

42

WHEN YOU WANT SOMETHING DESPERATELY ENOUGH, YOU MUST GO THE EXTRA MILE, AND DO WHAT NO ONE HAS DONE.

If you want a wonderful spouse you must begin to pray some kinds of prayer you have not been praying before.

42

WHEN YOU WANT SOMETHING DESPERATELY ENOUGH, YOU MUST GO THE EXTRA MILE, AND DO WHAT NO ONE HAS DONE.

If you want a wonderful spouse you must begin to pray some kinds of prayer you have not been praying before. Pray like Hannah who prayed a drunkard-type prayer and got her answer in the form of Samuel; pray like Jesus who sweated blood while on His kneels at Gethsemane; pray like Elijah who put his head between his knees and heavens opened and sent rain which had been withheld for three-and-half year. By the time you start praying these kinds of prayers, you will get what you desire (Matt.7:7-8).

43

WHEN GOD WANTS TO BLESS YOU, HE PUTS A PERSON IN YOUR LIFE.

When satan too wants to destroy one, he puts a person in his or her life using similar but reverse-destructive method.

WHEN GOD WANTS TO BLESS YOU, HE PUTS A PERSON IN YOUR LIFE.

God does not walk the streets dispensing money and marital breakthroughs to anybody who desires it. Any time God wants to bless someone, He sends a particular person his or her way. When satan too wants to destroy one, he puts a person in his or her life using similar but reverse-destructive method. This is the reason we taught in one of our previous volumes that, there are people you must pray to meet in life, and there are others you have to prophetically declare to miss, in order to get to your destined Promised Land. By praying the right kind of prayers, in line with the Will of God, things begin to happen in the spiritual realm in your favour. They may not materialize overnight, but with enduring patience, like that of the patriarch Job, they ultimately come to pass in wonderful forms that we never fathom.

44

SILENCE CAN NEVER BE MISQUOTED:

Follow the popular injunction: Silence
is golden, speech is silver.

SILENCE CAN NEVER BE MISQUOTED:

It is what you say that people will quote and use against you. Sometimes it is not necessary to say anything. It is best most times to remain silent and let events take divine shape. Follow the popular injunction: Silence is golden, speech is silver. It is wise for singles in courtship to heed the scriptural truth that, "quiet answer turns away wrath". When a partner in the relationship is angry, the other should be humble and wise enough to come down from his or her high horse till the heat of anger in the other person subsides.

45

A STINGY MAN WHO IS SINGLE WILL STILL BE STINGY WHEN MARRIED.

A bad habit is difficult to change in the confines of marriage.

A STINGY MAN WHO IS SINGLE WILL STILL BE STINGY WHEN MARRIED.

A leopard cannot change its spot; it will retain its natural colours whether dead or alive. A bad habit is difficult to change in the confines of marriage. For any man who is not teachable, or any lady who is not submissive enough, trying to change his or her behavior to make the marriage work is not worth investing time, money, energy and one's future on.

46

THREE WORDS THAT ECHO PEACE
IN MARRIAGE.

These are "I am sorry ",
"Thank you" and "I love you".

THREE WORDS THAT ECHO PEACE IN MARRIAGE.

There are three important words that blow the wholesome air of peace into any marriage. These are "I am sorry ", "Thank you" and "I love you". Start learning how to use these words now before you are married. Some men due to pride or arrogance will claim that they cannot utter these words. They are actually easy for anyone to say. All you need do is to just open your buccal cavity and let the words come forth, like Lazarus, from the orifice of your laryngeal tract. Your marriage will be the better for it.

47

DON'T WASTE YOUR TIME ON MEDITATING OR DWELLING ON YOUR SINGLENESS.

Adam was busy tending to the garden and grooming the animals when God brought Eve his way.

47

DON'T WASTE YOUR TIME ON MEDITATING OR DWELLING ON YOUR SINGLENESS.

Keep yourself busy doing something for the Lord while waiting for your divine partner. Adam was busy tending to the garden and grooming the animals when God brought Eve his way. Do not waste your precious time going to senseless parties or experimenting with worthless individuals. You need a quality time with the Lord while waiting for a marital breakthrough, very important.

48

CO-HABITATION IS A RECIPE FOR MARITAL FAILURE.

This is against the will of God for singles and it is a preparation for marital failure.

CO-HABITATION IS A RECIPE FOR MARITAL FAILURE.

Cohabitation is the act of a young man and a lady live together in an apartment, as husband and wife, whilst not legally married to each other. This is an immoral act which is rampant in many of our institutions of higher learning today. This is against the Will of God for singles and it is a preparation for marital failure. Most of these youths, apart from committing fornication, also end up committing the worse crime of abortion, which is unintentional murder as a result of this dangerous habit.

49

MASTURBATION IS DESTRUCTIVE.

Most of the prostitutes in the society today started out with the seemingly-innocuous act of masturbation.

MASTURBATION IS DESTRUCTIVE.

Masturbation is a dangerous habit. People often think it has no side-effect, but this is not the truth because it has a whole lot of effects. Research has shown that the results of masturbation will be harvested fifteen years after the act. There are both physical and spiritual effects. The physical effects for males include making the penis to be small, soft and flaccid. Masturbation will also make the penis bent and misshapen. It also leads to premature ejaculation, low sperm count and ultimately, impotency. The spiritual implication is that, whenever someone is masturbating, a spirit being or sexual demon is definitely involved and present because it is a perverse way of sexual act.

It should be noted that any act that attempts to topple the divine order is being sponsored and monitored by a strange spirit, and this is applicable to the repressible act of masturbation. The physical effects for ladies are that it makes them sexually unsatisfiable and could also lead to sexual looseness which can ultimately result into nymphomania. Most of the prostitutes in the society today started out with the seemingly-innocuous act of masturbation. The aggression with which the vagina and the clitoris are mal-handled during the perverse act makes it wear out easily. Fifteen years after, the womb would have been affected and a protruding stomach will be the result.

50

DEAL WITH ANTI-MARRIAGE DREAMS.

The devil and his agents use the channel of these bad dreams to introduce afflictions, sicknesses, delay, stagnation and retrogression into people's lives.

DEAL WITH ANTI-MARRIAGE DREAMS.

The enemy sometimes goes beyond the physical in order to attack the marital destiny of people. These are often carried out in the dream of such individuals. Some of such dreams are eating in the dream, sexual intercourse with known and unknown faces in the dream, seeing oneself in the market place, playing with unknown men and women, being pursued, stolen wedding garment, empty church during wedding ceremony, cases of partner being removed or disappearing beside one, disappearing shoes, disappearing wedding rings or gown, marriage with strange people in the dream, swimming in small or large bodies of waters, being raped or molested, marrying one's ex-lovers, taking examinations and not finishing it, going back to one's former school, house, office etc; seeing oneself naked, being romanced or kissed in the dream, seeing oneself pregnant, seeing men contesting for one's hand, marriage to relatives, seeing dead persons, and so on. The devil and his agents use the channel of these bad dreams to introduce afflictions, sicknesses, delay, stagnation and retrogression into people's lives.

These dreams should be nullified and rendered ineffective through the potency of the blood of Jesus, for doors of breakthroughs and abundant life and prosperity in Christ to be lived and enjoyed.

www.ingramcontent.com/pod-product-compliance
Lightning Source LLC
La Vergne TN
LVHW051247080426
835513LV00016B/1793